A Trampwoman's Tragedy

THOMAS HARDY

A Phoenix Paperback

Selected Poems by Thomas Hardy
first published by J. M. Dent in 1994
Selected Short Stories and Poems by Thomas Hardy
first published by J. M. Dent in 1992

This abridged edition published in 1996 by Phoenix
a division of Orion Books Ltd
Orion House, 5 Upper St Martin's Lane, London WC2H 9EA

Cover illustration: *A Shady Spot*, by George Laugee, Whitford & Hughes,
London (Bridgeman Art Library, London)

ISBN 1 85799 663 1

Typeset by Deltatype Ltd, Ellesmere Port, Cheshire
Printed and bound in Great Britain by
Clays Ltd, St Ives plc

CONTENTS

A Trampwoman's Tragedy

I

From Wynyard's Gap the livelong day,
    The livelong day,
We beat afoot the northward way
    We had travelled times before.
The sun-blaze burning on our backs,
Our shoulders sticking to our packs,
By fosseway, fields, and turnpike tracks
    We skirted sad Sedge-Moor.

2

Full twenty miles we jaunted on,
    We jaunted on, –
My fancy-man, and jeering John,
    And Mother Lee, and I.
And, as the sun drew down to west,
We climbed the toilsome Poldon crest,
And saw, of landskip sights the best,
    The inn that beamed thereby.

3

For months we had padded side by side,
    Ay, side by side
Through the Great Forest, Blackmoor wide,

And where the Parret ran.
We'd faced the gusts on Mendip ridge,
Had crossed the Yeo unhelped by bridge,
Been stung by every Marshwood midge,
    I and my fancy-man.

4

Lone inns we loved, my man and I,
    My man and I;
'King's Stag', 'Windwhistle' high and dry,
    'The Horse' on Hintock Green,
The cosy house at Wynyard's Gap,
'The Hut' renowned on Bredy Knap,
And many another wayside tap
    Where folk might sit unseen.

5

Now as we trudged – O deadly day,
    O deadly day! –
I teased my fancy-man in play
    And wanton idleness.
I walked alongside jeering John,
I laid his hand my waist upon;
I would not bend my glances on
    My lover's dark distress.

6

Thus Poldon top at last we won,
    At last we won,
And gained the inn at sink of sun
    Far-famed as 'Marshal's Elm'.
Beneath us figured tor and lea,
From Mendip to the western sea –
I doubt if finer sight there be
    Within this royal realm.

7

Inside the settle all a-row –
    All four a-row
We sat, I next to John, to show
    That he had wooed and won.
And then he took me on his knee,
And swore it was his turn to be
My favoured mate, and Mother Lee
    Passed to my former one.

8

Then in a voice I had never heard,
    I had never heard,
My only Love to me: 'One word,
    My lady, if you please!
Whose is the child you are like to bear? –
His? After all my months o' care?'
God knows 'twas not! But, O despair!
    I nodded – still to tease.

Then up he sprung, and with his knife –
    And with his knife
He let out jeering Johnny's life,
    Yes; there, at set of sun.
The slant ray through the window nigh
Gilded John's blood and glazing eye,
Ere scarcely Mother Lee and I
    Knew that the deed was done.

The taverns tell the gloomy tale,
    The gloomy tale,
How that at Ivel-chester jail
    My Love, my sweetheart swung;
Though stained till now by no misdeed
Save one horse ta'en in time o' need;
(Blue Jimmy stole right many a steed
    Ere his last fling he flung.)

Thereaft I walked the world alone,
    Alone, alone!
On his death-day I gave my groan.
    And dropt his dead-born child.
'Twas nigh the jail, beneath a tree,
None tending me; for Mother Lee
Had died at Glaston, leaving me
    Unfriended on the wild.

And in the night as I lay weak,
    As I lay weak,
The leaves a-falling on my cheek,
    The red moon low declined –
The ghost of him I'd die to kiss
Rose up and said: 'Ah, tell me this!
Was the child mine, or was it his?
    Speak, that I rest may find!'

O doubt not but I told him then,
    I told him then,
That I had kept me from all men
    Since we joined lips and swore.
Whereat he smiled, and thinned away
As the wind stirred to call up day . . .
– 'Tis past! And here alone I stray
    Haunting the Western Moor.

Her Death and After

The summons was urgent: and forth I went –
By the way of the Western Wall, so drear
On that winter night, and sought a gate,
    Where one, by Fate,
    Lay dying that I held dear.

And there, as I paused by her tenement,
And the trees shed on me their rime and hoar,
I thought of the man who had left her lone –
      Him who made her his own
  When I loved her, long before.

The rooms within had the piteous shine
That home-things wear when there's aught amiss;
From the stairway floated the rise and fall
      Of an infant's call,
  Whose birth had brought her to this.

Her life was the price she would pay for that whine –
For a child by the man she did not love.
'But let that rest for ever,' I said,
      And bent my tread
  To the bedchamber above.

She took my hand in her thin white own,
And smiled her thanks – though nigh too weak –
And made them a sign to leave us there,
      Then faltered, ere
  She could bring herself to speak.

'Just to see you – before I go – he'll condone
Such a natural thing now my time's not much –
When Death is so near it hustles hence
      All passioned sense
  Between woman and man as such!

'My husband is absent. As heretofore
The City detains him. But, in truth,
He has not been kind . . . I will speak no blame,
     But – the child is lame;
  O, I pray she may reach his ruth!

'Forgive past days – I can say no more –
Maybe had we wed you would now repine! . . .
But I treated you ill. I was punished. Farewell!
     – Truth shall I tell?
  Would the child were yours and mine!

'As a wife I was true. But, such my unease
That, could I insert a deed back in Time,
I'd make her yours, to secure your care;
     And the scandal bear,
  And the penalty for the crime!'

– When I had left, and the swinging trees
Rang above me, as lauding her candid say,
Another was I. Her words were enough:
     Came smooth, came rough,
  I felt I could live my day.

Next night she died; and her obsequies
In the Field of Tombs where the earthworks frowned
Had her husband's heed. His tendance spent,
     I often went
  And pondered by her mound.

All that year and the next year whiled,
And I still went thitherward in the gloom;
But the Town forgot her and her nook,
And her husband took
Another Love to his home.

And the rumour flew that the lame lone child
Whom she wished for its safety child of mine,
Was treated ill when offspring came
Of the new-made dame,
And marked a more vigorous line.

A smarter grief within me wrought
Than even at loss of her so dear –
That the being whose soul my soul suffused
Had a child ill-used,
While I dared not interfere!

One eve as I stood at my spot of thought
In the white-stoned Garth, brooding thus her wrong,
Her husband neared; and to shun his nod
By her hallowed sod
I went from the tombs among

To the Cirque of the Gladiators which faced –
That haggard mark of Imperial Rome,
Whose Pagan echoes mock the chime
Of our Christian time
From its hollows of chalk and loam.

The sun's gold touch was scarce displaced
From the vast Arena where men once bled,
When her husband followed; bowed; half-passed
      With lip upcast;
    Then halting sullenly said:

'It is noised that you visit my first wife's tomb.
Now, I gave her an honoured name to bear
While living, when dead. So I've claim to ask
      By what right you task
    My patience by vigiling there?

'There's a decency even in death, I assume;
Preserve it, sir, and keep away;
For the mother of my first-born you
      Show mind undue!
    – Sir, I've nothing more to say.'

A desperate stroke discerned I then –
God pardon – or pardon not – the lie;
She had sighed that she wished (lest the child should pine
      Of slights) 'twere mine,
    So I said: 'But the father I.

'That you thought it yours is the way of men;
But I won her troth long ere your day:

You learnt how, in dying, she summoned me?
                'Twas in fealty.
        – Sir, I've nothing more to say,

'Save that, if you'll hand me my little maid,
I'll take her, and rear her, and spare you toil.
Think it more than a friendly act none can;
                I'm a lonely man,
        While you've a large pot to boil.

'If not, and you'll put it to ball or blade –
To-night, to-morrow night, anywhen –
I'll meet you here. . . . But think of it,
                And in season fit
        Let me hear from you again.'

– Well, I went away, hoping; but nought I heard
Of my stroke for the child, till there greeted me
A little voice that one day came
                To my window-frame
        And babbled innocently:

'My father who's not my own, sends word
I'm here to stay here, sir, where I belong!'
Next a writing came: 'Since the child was the fruit
                Of your lawless suit,
        Pray take her, to right a wrong.'

And I did. And I gave the child my love,
And the child loved me, and estranged us none.
But compunctions loomed; for I'd harmed the dead
      By what I said
    For the good of the living one.

– Yet though, God wot, I am sinner enough,
And unworthy the woman who drew me so,
Perhaps this wrong for her darling's good
      She forgives, or would,
    If only she could know!

Drummer Hodge

I

They throw in Drummer Hodge, to rest
    Uncoffined – just as found:
His landmark is a kopje-crest
    That breaks the veldt around;
And foreign constellations west
    Each night above his mound.

2

Young Hodge the Drummer never knew –
    Fresh from his Wessex home –
The meaning of the broad Karoo,
    The Bush, the dusty loam,

And why uprose to nightly view
    Strange stars amid the gloom.

3

Yet portion of that unknown plain
    Will Hodge for ever be;
His homely Northern breast and brain
    Grow to some Southern tree,
And strange-eyed constellations reign
    His stars eternally.

A Broken Appointment

You did not come,
And marching Time drew on, and wore me numb. –
Yet less for loss of your dear presence there
Than that I thus found lacking in your make
That high compassion which can overbear
Reluctance for pure lovingkindness' sake
Grieved I, when, as the hope-hour stroked its sum,
You did not come.

You love me not,
And love alone can lend you loyalty;
– I know and knew it. But, unto the store
Of human deeds divine in all but name,
Was it not worth a little hour or more

To add yet this: Once you, a woman, came
To soothe a time-torn man; even though it be
            You love not me?

An August Midnight

1

A shaded lamp and a waving blind,
And the beat of a clock from a distant floor:
On this scene enter – winged, horned, and spined –
A longlegs, a moth, and a dumbledore;
While 'mid my page there idly stands
A sleepy fly, that rubs its hands . . .

2

Thus meet we five, in this still place,
At this point of time, at this point in space.
– My guests besmear my new-penned line,
Or bang at the lamp and fall supine.
'God's humblest, they!' I muse. Yet why?
They know Earth-secrets that know not I.

The Darkling Thrush

I leant upon a coppice gate
    When Frost was spectre-gray,
And Winter's dregs made desolate
    The weakening eye of day.
The tangled bine-stems scored the sky
    Like strings of broken lyres,
And all mankind that haunted nigh
    Had sought their household fires.

The land's sharp features seemed to be
    The Century's corpse outleant,
His crypt the cloudy canopy,
    The wind his death-lament.
The ancient pulse of germ and birth
    Was shrunken hard and dry,
And every spirit upon earth
    Seemed fervourless as I.

At once a voice arose among
    The bleak twigs overhead
In a full-hearted evensong
    Of joy illimited;
An aged thrush, frail, gaunt, and small,
    In blast-beruffled plume,
Had chosen thus to fling his soul
    Upon the growing gloom.

So little cause for carolings
    Of such ecstatic sound
Was written on terrestrial things
    Afar or nigh around,
That I could think there trembled through
    His happy good-night air
Some blessed Hope, whereof he knew
    And I was unaware.

The Self-Unseeing

Here is the ancient floor,
Footworn and hollowed and thin,
Here was the former door
Where the dead feet walked in.

She sat here in her chair,
Smiling into the fire;
He who played stood there,
Bowing it higher and higher.

Childlike, I danced in a dream;
Blessings emblazoned that day;
Everything glowed with a gleam;
Yet we were looking away!

Shut Out That Moon

Close up the casement, draw the blind,
    Shut out that stealing moon,
She wears too much the guise she wore
    Before our lutes were strewn
With years-deep dust, and names we read
    On a white stone were hewn.

Step not forth on the dew-dashed lawn
    To view the Lady's Chair,
Immense Orion's glittering form,
    The Less and Greater Bear:
Stay in; to such sights we were dràwn
    When faded ones were fair.

Brush not the bough for midnight scents
    That come forth lingeringly,
And wake the same sweet sentiments
    They breathed to you and me
When living seemed a laugh, and love
    All it was said to be.

Within the common lamp-lit room
    Prison my eyes and thought;
Let dingy details crudely loom,
    Mechanic speech be wrought:
Too fragrant was Life's early bloom,
    Too tart the fruit it brought!

A Church Romance

She turned in the high pew, until her sight
Swept the west gallery, and caught its row
Of music-men with viol, book, and bow
Against the sinking sad tower-window light.

She turned again; and in her pride's despite
One strenuous viol's inspirer seemed to throw
A message from his string to her below,
Which said: 'I claim thee as my own forthright!'

Thus their hearts' bond began, in due time signed.
And long years thence, when Age had scared Romance,
At some old attitude of his or glance
That gallery-scene would break upon her mind,
With him as minstrel, ardent, young, and trim,
Bowing 'New Sabbath' or 'Mount Ephraim'.

The Convergence of the Twain

(Lines on the loss of the 'Titanic')

I

In a solitude of the sea
Deep from human vanity,
And the Pride of Life that planned her, stilly couches she.

17

2

Steel chambers, late the pyres
Of her salamandrine fires,
Cold currents thrid, and turn to rhythmic tidal lyres.

3

Over the mirrors meant
To glass the opulent
The sea-worm crawls – grotesque, slimed, dumb, indifferent.

4

Jewels in joy designed
To ravish the sensuous mind
Lie lightless, all their sparkles bleared and black and blind.

5

Dim moon-eyed fishes near
Gaze at the gilded gear
And query: 'What does this vaingloriousness down here?' . . .

6

Well: while was fashioning
This cretaure of cleaving wing,
The Immanent Will that stirs and urges everything

7

Prepared a sinister mate
For her – so gaily great –
A Shape of Ice, for the time far and dissociate.

8

And as the smart ship grew
In stature, grace, and hue,
In shadowy silent distance grew the Iceberg too.

9

Alien they seemed to be:
No mortal eye could see
The intimate welding of their later history,

10

Or sign that they were bent
By paths coincident
On being anon twin halves of one august event,

11

Till the Spinner of the Years
Said 'Now!' And each one hears,
And consummation comes, and jars two hemispheres.

My Spirit Will Not Haunt the Mound

My spirit will not haunt the mound
    Above my breast,
But travel, memory-possessed,
To where my tremulous being found
    Life largest, best.

My phantom-footed shape will go
    When nightfall grays
Hither and thither along the ways
I and another used to know
    In backward days.

And there you'll find me, if a jot
    You still should care
For me, and for my curious air;
If otherwise, then I shall not,
    For you, be there.

The Going

Why did you give no hint that night
That quickly after the morrow's dawn,
And calmly, as if indifferent quite,
You would close your term here, up and be gone
    Where I could not follow

With wing of swallow
To gain one glimpse of you ever anon!

Never to bid good-bye,
Or lip me the softest call,
Or utter a wish for a word, while I
Saw morning harden upon the wall,
Unmoved, unknowing
That your great going
Had place that moment, and altered all.

Why do you make me leave the house
And think for a breath it is you I see
At the end of the alley of bending boughs
Where so often at dusk you used to be;
Till in darkening dankness
The yawning blankness
Of the perspective sickens me!

You were she who abode
By those red-veined rocks far West,
You were the swan-necked one who rode
Along the beetling Beeny Crest,
And, reining nigh me,
Would muse and eye me,
While life unrolled us its very best.

Why, then, latterly did we not speak,

Did we not think of those days long dead,
And ere your vanishing strive to seek
That time's renewal? We might have said,
      'In this bright spring weather
      We'll visit together
Those places that once we visited.'

      Well, well! All's past amend,
      Unchangeable. It must go.
I seem but a dead man held on end
To sink down soon . . . O you could not know
      That such swift fleeing
      No soul foreseeing –
Not even I – would undo me so!

Your Last Drive

Here by the moorway you returned,
And saw the borough lights ahead
That lit your face – all undiscerned
To be in a week the face of the dead,
And you told of the charm of that haloed view
That never again would beam on you.

And on your left you passed the spot
Where eight days later you were to lie,
And be spoken of as one who was not;

Beholding it with a heedless eye
As alien from you, though under its tree
You soon would halt everlastingly.

I drove not with you . . . Yet had I sat
At your side that eve I should not have seen
That the countenance I was glancing at
Had a last-time look in the flickering sheen,
Nor have read the writing upon your face,
'I go hence soon to my resting-place;

'You may miss me then. But I shall not know
How many times you visit me there,
Or what your thoughts are, or if you go
There never at all. And I shall not care.
Should you censure me I shall take no heed,
And even your praises no more shall need.'

True: never you'll know. And you will not mind
But shall I then slight you because of such?
Dear ghost, in the past did you ever find
The thought 'What profit,' move me much?
Yet abides the fact, indeed, the same, –
You are past love, praise, indifference, blame.

The Walk

You did not walk with me
Of late to the hill-top tree
    By the gated ways,
    As in earlier days;
    You were weak and lame,
    So you never came,
And I went alone, and I did not mind,
Not thinking of you as left behind.

I walked up there to-day
Just in the former way;
    Surveyed around
    The familiar ground
    By myself again:
    What difference, then?
Only that underlying sense
Of the look of a room on returning thence.

Rain on a Grave

Clouds spout upon her
    Their waters amain
    In ruthless disdain, –
Her who but lately
    Had shivered with pain

As at touch of dishonour
If there had lit on her
So coldly, so straightly
    Such arrows of rain:

One who to shelter
    Her delicate head
Would quicken and quicken
    Each tentative tread
If drops chanced to pelt her
    That summertime spills
    In dust-paven rills
When thunder-clouds thicken
    And birds close their bills.

Would that I lay there
    And she were housed here!
Or better, together
Were folded away there
Exposed to one weather
We both, – who would stray there
When sunny the day there,
    Or evening was clear
    At the prime of the year.

Soon will be growing
    Green blades from her mound,
And daisies be showing

Like stars on the ground,
Till she form part of them –
Ay – the sweet heart of them,
Loved beyond measure
With a child's pleasure
    All her life's round.

I Found Her Out There

I found her out there
On a slope few see,
That falls westwardly
To the salt-edged air,
Where the ocean breaks
On the purple strand,
And the hurricane shakes
The solid land.

I brought her here,
And have laid her to rest
In a noiseless nest
No sea beats near.
She will never be stirred
In her loamy cell
By the waves long heard
And loved so well.

So she does not sleep
By those haunted heights
The Atlantic smites
And the blind gales sweep,
Whence she often would gaze
At Dundagel's famed head,
While the dipping blaze
Dyed her face fire-red;

And would sigh at the tale
Of sunk Lyonnesse,
As a wind-tugged tress
Flapped her cheek like a flail;
Or listen at whiles
With a thought-bound brow
To the murmuring miles
She is far from now.

Yet her shade, maybe,
Will creep underground
Till it catch the sound
Of that western sea
As it swells and sobs
Where she once domiciled,
And joy in its throbs
With the heart of a child.

Without Ceremony

It was your way, my dear,
To vanish without a word
When callers, friends, or kin
Had left, and I hastened in
To rejoin you, as I inferred.

And when you'd a mind to career
Off anywhere – say to town –
You were all on a sudden gone
Before I had thought thereon,
Or noticed your trunks were down.

So, now that you disappear
For ever in that swift style,
Your meaning seems to me
Just as it used to be:
'Good-bye is not worth while!'

Lament

How she would have loved
A party to-day! –
Bright-hatted and gloved,
With table and tray
And chairs on the lawn

Her smiles would have shone
With welcomings . . . But
She is shut, she is shut
  From friendship's spell
  In the jailing shell
  Of her tiny cell.

Or she would have reigned
At a dinner to-night
With ardours unfeigned,
And a generous delight;
All in her abode
She'd have freely bestowed
On her guests . . . But alas,
She is shut under grass
  Where no cups flow,
  Powerless to know
  That it might be so.

And she would have sought
With a child's eager glance
The shy snowdrops brought
By the new year's advance,
And peered in the rime
Of Candlemas-time
For crocuses . . . chanced
It that she were not tranced
  From sights she loved best;

Wholly possessed
By an infinite rest!

And we are here staying
Amid these stale things,
Who care not for gaying,
And those junketings
That used so to joy her,
And never to cloy her
As us they cloy! . . . But
She is shut, she is shut
From the cheer of them, dead
To all done and said
In her yew-arched bed.

The Haunter

He does not think that I haunt here nightly:
    How shall I let him know
That whither his fancy sets him wandering
    I, too, alertly go? –
Hover and hover a few feet from him
    Just as I used to do,
But cannot answer the words he lifts me –
    Only listen thereto!

When I could answer he did not say them:

When I could let him know
How I would like to join in his journeys
Seldom he wished to go.
Now that he goes and wants me with him
More than he used to do,
Never he sees my faithful phantom
Though he speaks thereto.

Yes, I companion him to places
Only dreamers know,
Where the shy hares print long paces,
Where the night rooks go;
Into old aisles where the past is all to him,
Close as his shade can do,
Always lacking the power to call to him,
Near as I reach thereto!

What a good haunter I am, O tell him!
Quickly make him know
If he but sigh since my loss befell him
Straight to his side I go.
Tell him a faithful one is doing
All that love can do
Still that his path may be worth pursuing,
And to bring peace thereto.

The Voice

Woman much missed, how you call to me, call to me,
Saying that now you are not as you were
When you had changed from the one who was all to me,
But as at first, when our day was fair.

Can it be you that I hear? Let me view you, then,
Standing as when I drew near to the town
Where you would wait for me: yes, as I knew you then,
Even to the original air-blue gown!

Or is it only the breeze, in its listlessness
Travelling across the wet mead to me here,
You being ever dissolved to wan wistlessness,
Heard no more again far or near?

    Thus I; faltering forward,
    Leaves around me falling,
Wind oozing thin through the thorn from norward,
    And the woman calling.

After a Journey

Hereto I come to view a voiceless ghost;
    Whither, O whither will its whim now draw me?
Up the cliff, down, till I'm lonely, lost,

And the unseen waters' ejaculations awe me.
Where you will next be there's no knowing,
    Facing round about me everywhere,
        With your nut-coloured hair,
And gray eyes, and rose-flush coming and going.

Yes: I have re-entered your olden haunts at last;
    Through the years, through the dead scenes I have tracked
        you
What have you now found to say of our past –
    Scanned across the dark space wherein I have lacked you?
Summer gave us sweets, but autumn wrought division?
    Things were not lastly as firstly well
        With us twain, you tell?
But all's closed now, despite Time's derision.

I see what you are doing: you are leading me on
    To the spots we knew when we haunted here together,
The waterfall, above which the mist-bow shone
    At the then fair hour in the then fair weather,
And the cave just under, with a voice still so hollow
    That it seems to call out to me from forty years ago,
        When you were all aglow,
And not the thin ghost that I now frailly follow!

Ignorant of what there is flitting here to see,
    The waked birds preen and the seals flop lazily;
Soon you will have, Dear, to vanish from me,

For the stars close their shutters and the dawn whitens
   hazily.
Trust me, I mind not, though Life lours,
   The bringing me here; nay, bring me here again!
      I am just the same as when
Our days were a joy, and our paths through flowers.

Beeny Cliff

1

O the opal and the sapphire of that wandering western sea,
And the woman riding high above with bright hair flapping
   free –
The woman whom I loved so, and who loyally loved me.

2

The pale mews plained below us, and the waves seemed far
   away
In a nether sky, engrossed in saying their ceaseless babbling
   say,
As we laughed light-heartedly aloft on that clear-sunned
   March day.

3

A little cloud then cloaked us, and there flew an irised rain,
And the Atlantic dyed its levels with a dull misfeatured
   stain,

And then the sun burst out again, and purples prinked the
main.

4

– Still in all its chasmal beauty bulks old Beeny to the sky,
And shall she and I not go there once again now March is
nigh,
And the sweet things said in that March say anew there by
and by?

5

What if still in chasmal beauty looms that wild weird
western shore,
The woman now is – elsewhere – whom the ambling pony
bore,
And nore knows nor cares for Beeny, and will laugh there
nevermore.

At Castle Boterel

As I drive to the junction of lane and highway,
    And the drizzle bedrenches the waggonette,
I look behind at the fading byway,
    And see on its slope, now glistening wet,
        Distinctly yet

Myself and a girlish form benighted

In dry March weather. We climb the road
Beside a chaise. We had just alighted
    To ease the sturdy pony's load
        When he sighed and slowed.

What we did as we climbed, and what we talked of
    Matters not much, nor to what it led, –
Something that life will not be balked of
    Without rude reason till hope is dead,
        And feeling fled.

It filled but a minute. But was there ever
    A time of such quality, since or before,
In that hill's story? To one mind never,
    Though it has been climbed, foot-swift, foot-sore,
        By thousands more.

Primaeval rocks form the road's steep border,
    And much have they faced there, first and last,
Of the transitory in Earth's long order;
    But what they record in colour and cast
        Is – that we two passed.

And to me, though Time's unflinching rigour,
    In mindless rote, has ruled from sight
The substance now, one phantom figure
    Remains on the slope, as when that night
        Saw us alight.

I look and see it there, shrinking, shrinking,
   I look back at it amid the rain
For the very last time; for my sand is sinking,
   And I shall traverse old love's domain
     Never again.

The Phantom Horsewoman

I

Queer are the ways of a man I know:
   He comes and stands
   In a careworn craze,
   And looks at the sands
   And the seaward haze
   With moveless hands
   And face and gaze,
   Then turns to go . . .
And what does he see when he gazes so?

2

They say he sees as an instant thing
   More clear than to-day,
   A sweet soft scene
   That was once in play
   By that briny green;
   Yes, notes alway
   Warm, real, and keen,

What his black years bring –
A phantom of his own figuring.

3

Of this vision of his they might say more:
    Not only there
    Does he see this sight,
    But everywhere
    In his brain – day, night,
    As if on the air
    It were drawn rose bright –
    Yea, far from that shore
Does he carry this vision of heretofore:

4

A ghost-girl-rider. And though, toil-tried,
    He withers daily,
    Time touches her not,
    But she still rides gaily
    In his rapt thought
    On that shagged and shaly
    Atlantic spot,
    And as when first eyed
Draws rein and sings to the swing of the tide.

Afternoon Service at Mellstock

On afternoons of drowsy calm
    We stood in the panelled pew,
Singing one-voiced a Tate-and-Brady psalm
    To the tune of 'Cambridge New'.

We watched the elms, we watched the rooks,
    The clouds upon the breeze,
Between the whiles of glancing at our books,
    And swaying like the trees.

So mindless were those outpourings! –
    Though I am not aware
That I have gained by subtle thought on things
    Since we stood psalming there.

The Oxen

Christmas Eve, and twelve of the clock.
    'Now they are all on their knees,'
An elder said as we sat in a flock
    By the embers in hearthside ease.

We pictured the meek mild creatures where
    They dwelt in their strawy pen,
Nor did it occur to one of us there
    To doubt they were kneeling then.

So fair a fancy few would weave
    In these years! Yet, I feel,
If someone said on Christmas Eve,
    'Come; see the oxen kneel

'In the lonely barton by yonder coomb
    Our childhood used to know,'
I should go with him in the gloom,
    Hoping it might be so.

Old Furniture

I know not how it may be with others
    Who sit amid relics of householdry
That date from the days of their mothers' mothers,
    But well I know how it is with me
      Continually.

I see the hands of the generations
    That owned each shiny familiar thing
In play on its knobs and indentations,
    And with its ancient fashioning
      Still dallying:

Hands behind hands, growing paler and paler,
    As in a mirror a candle-flame

Shows images of itself, each frailer
    As it recedes, though the eye may frame
        Its shape the same.

On the clock's dull dial a foggy finger,
    Moving to set the minutes right
With tentative touches that lift and linger
    In the wont of a moth on a summer night,
        Creeps to my sight.

On this old viol, too, fingers are dancing –
    As whilom – just over the strings by the nut,
The tip of a bow receding, advancing
    In airy quivers, as if it would cut
        The plaintive gut.

And I see a face by that box for tinder,
    Glowing forth in fits from the dark,
And fading again, as the linten cinder
    Kindles to red at the flinty spark,
        Or goes out stark.

Well, well. It is best to be up and doing,
    The world has no use for one to-day
Who eyes things thus – no aim pursuing!
    He should not continue in this stay,
        But sink away.

During Wind and Rain

They sing their dearest songs –
He, she, all of them – yea,
Treble and tenor and bass,
   And one to play;
With the candles mooning each face . . .
   Ah, no; the years O!
How the sick leaves reel down in throngs!

They clear the creeping moss –
Elders and juniors – aye,
Making the pathways neat
   And the garden gay;
And they build a shady seat . . .
   Ah, no; the years, the years;
See, the white storm-birds wing across!

They are blithely breakfasting all –
Men and maidens – yea,
Under the summer tree,
   With a glimpse of the bay,
While pet fowl come to the knee . . .
   Ah, no; the years O!
And the rotten rose is ript from the wall.

They change to a high new house,
He, she, all of them – aye,

Clocks, and carpets and chairs
   On the lawn all day,
And brightest things that are theirs . . .
   Ah, no; the years, the years;
Down their carved names the rain-drop ploughs.

Midnight on the Great Western

In the third-class seat sat the journeying boy,
   And the roof-lamp's oily flame
Played down on his listless form and face,
Bewrapt past knowing to what he was going,
   Or whence he came.

In the band of his hat the journeying boy
   Had a ticket stuck; and a string
Around his neck bore the key of his box,
That twinkled gleams of the lamp's sad beams
   Like a living thing.

What past can be yours, O journeying boy
   Towards a world unknown,
Who calmly, as if incurious quite
On all at stake, can undertake
   This plunge alone?

Knows your soul a sphere, O journeying boy

Our rude realms far above,
Whence with spacious vision you mark and mete
This region of sin that you find you in,
But are not of?

In Time of 'The Breaking of Nations'

I

Only a man harrowing clods
   In a slow silent walk
With an old horse that stumbles and nods
   Half asleep as they stalk.

2

Only thin smoke without flame
   From the heaps of couch-grass;
Yet this will go onward the same
   Though Dynasties pass.

3

Yonder a maid and her wight
   Come whispering by:
War's annals will cloud into night
   Ere their story die.

Afterwards

When the Present has latched its postern behind my
    tremulous stay,
  And the May month flaps its glad green leaves like wings,
Delicate-filmed as new-spun silk, will the neighbours say,
  'He was a man who used to notice such things'?

If it be in the dusk when, like an eyelid's soundless blink,
  The dewfall-hawk comes crossing the shades to alight
Upon the wind-harped upland thorn, a gazer may think,
  'To him this must have been a familiar sight.'

If I pass during some nocturnal blackness, mothy and
    warm,
  When the hedgehog travels furtively over the lawn
One may say, 'He strove that such innocent creatures
    should come to no harm,
  But he could do little for them; and now he is gone.'

If, when hearing that I have been stilled at last, they stand at
    the door,
  Watching the full-starred heavens that winter sees,
Will this thought rise on those who will meet my face no
    more,
  'He was one who had an eye for such mysteries'?

And will any say when my bell of quittance is heard in the
    gloom,

And a crossing breeze cuts a pause in its outrollings,
Till they rise again, as they were a new bell's boom,
'He hears it not now, but used to notice such things'?

Weathers

1

This is the weather the cuckoo likes,
    And so do I;
When showers betumble the chestnut spikes,
    And nestlings fly:
And the little brown nightingale bills his best,
And they sit outside at 'The Travellers' Rest',
And maids come forth sprig-muslin drest,
And citizens dream of the south and west,
    And so do I.

2

This is the weather the shepherd shuns,
    And so do I;
When beeches drip in browns and duns,
    And thresh, and ply;
And hill-hid tides throb, throe on throe,
And meadow rivulets overflow,
And drops on gate-bars hang in a row,
And rooks in families homeward go,
    And so do I.

The Fallow Dear at the Lonely House

One without looks in to-night
    Through the curtain-chink
From the sheet of glistening white;
One without looks in to-night
    As we sit and think
      By the fender-brink.

We do not discern those eyes
    Watching in the snow;
Lit by lamps of rosy dyes
We do not discern those eyes
    Wondering, aglow,
      Fourfooted, tiptoe.

'A Gentleman's Second-Hand Suit'

Here it is hanging in the sun
    By the pawn-shop door,
A dress-suit – all its revels done
    Of heretofore.
Long drilled to the waltzers' swing and sway,
    As its tokens show:
What it has seen, what it could say
    If it did but know!

The sleeve bears still a print of powder
      Rubbed from her arms
When she warmed up as the notes swelled louder
      And livened her charms –
Or rather theirs, for beauties many
      Leant there, no doubt,
Leaving these tell-tale traces when he
      Spun them about.

Its cut seems rather in bygone style
      On looking close,
So it mayn't have bent it for some while
      To the dancing pose:
Anyhow, often within its clasp
      Fair partners hung,
Assenting to the wearer's grasp
      With soft sweet tongue.

Where is, alas, the gentleman
      Who wore this suit?
And where are his ladies? Tell none can:
      Gossip is mute.
Some of them may forget him quite
      Who smudged his sleeve,
Some think of a wild and whirling night
      With him, and grieve.

That Kiss in the Dark

>   Recall it you? –
>   Say you do! –
> When you went out into the night,
> In an impatience that would not wait,
> From that lone house in the woodland spot,
> And when I, thinking you had gone
> For ever and ever from my sight,
> Came after, printing a kiss upon
>   Black air
>   In my despair,
> And my two lips lit on your cheek
> As you leant silent against a gate,
> Making my woman's face flush hot
> At what I had done in the dark, unaware
> You lingered for me but would not speak:
> Yes, kissed you, thinking you were not there!
>   Recall it you? –
>   Say you do!

Domicilium

It faces west, and round the back and sides
High beeches, bending, hang a veil of boughs,
And sweep against the roof. Wild honeysucks
Climb on the walls, and seem to sprout a wish

(If we may fancy wish of trees and plants)
To overtop the apple-trees hard by.

Red roses, lilacs, variegated box
Are there in plenty, and such hardy flowers
As flourish best untrained. Adjoining these
Are herbs and esculents; and farther still
A field; then cottages with trees, and last
The distant hills and sky.

Behind, the scene is wilder. Heath and furze
Are everything that seems to grow and thrive
Upon the uneven ground. A stunted thorn
Stands here and there, indeed; and from a pit
An oak uprises, springing from a seed
Dropped by some bird a hundred years ago.

                      In days bygone –
Long gone – my father's mother, who is now
Blest with the blest, would take me out to walk.
At such a time I once inquired of her
How looked the spot when first she settled here.
The answer I remember. 'Fifty years
Have passed since then, my child, and change has marked
The face of all things. Yonder garden-plots
And orchards were uncultivated slopes
O'ergrown with bramble bushes, furze and thorn:
That road a narrow path shut in by ferns,
Which, almost trees, obscured the passer-by.

The Night of Trafalgár

(Boatman's Song)

1

In the wild October night-time, when the wind raved round
    the land,
And the Back-sea met the Front-sea, and our doors were
    blocked with sand,
And we heard the drub of Dead-man's Bay, where bones of
    thousands are,
We knew not what the day had done for us at Trafalgár.
               Had done,
               Had done,
         For us at Trafalgár!

2

'Pull hard, and make the Nothe, or down we go!' one says,
    says he.
We pulled; and bedtime brought the storm; but snug at
    home slept we.
Yet all the while our gallants after fighting through the day,
Were beating up and down the dark, sou'-west of Cadiz
    Bay.
               The dark,
               The dark,
         Sou'-west of Cadiz Bay!

The victors and the vanquished then the storm it tossed and
    tore,
As hard they strove, those worn-out men, upon that surly
    shore;
Dead Nelson and his half-dead crew, his foes from near and
    far,
Were rolled together on the deep that night at Trafalgár!
            The deep,
            The deep,
        That night at Trafalgár!

Budmouth Dears

(Hussar's Song)

1

When we lay where Budmouth Beach is,
    O, the girls were fresh as peaches,
With their tall and tossing figures and their eyes of blue and
    brown!
And our hearts would ache with longing
As we paced from our sing-songing,
With a smart *Clink! Clink!* up the Esplanade and down.

2

They distracted and delayed us

By the pleasant pranks they played us,
And what marvel, then, if troopers, even of regiments of
   renown
   On whom flashed those eyes divine, O,
   Should forget the countersign, O,
As we tore *Clink! Clink!* back to camp above the town.

3

   Do they miss us much, I wonder
   Now that war has swept us sunder,
And we roam from where the faces smile to where the faces
   frown?
   And no more behold the features
   Of the fair fantastic creatures,
And no more *Clink! Clink!* past the parlours of the town?

4

   Shall we once again there meet them?
   Falter fond attempts to greet them?
Will the gay sling-jacket glow again beside the muslin
   gown? –
   Will they archly quiz and con us
   With a sideway glance upon us,
While our spurs *Clink! Clink!* up the Esplanade and down?

The Eve of Waterloo

(Chorus of Phantoms)

The eyelids of eve fall together at last,
And the forms so foreign to field and tree
Lie down as though native, and slumber fast!

Sore are the thrills of misgiving we see
In the artless champaign at this harlequinade,
Distracting a vigil where calm should be!

The green seems opprest, and the Plain afraid
Of a Something to come, whereof these are the proofs, –
Neither earthquake, nor storm, nor eclipse's shade!

Yea, the coneys are scared by the thud of hoofs,
And their white scuts flash at their vanishing heels,
And swallows abandon the hamlet-roofs.

The mole's tunnelled chambers are crushed by wheels,
The lark's eggs scattered, their owners fled;
And the hedgehog's household the sapper unseals.

The snail draws in at the terrible tread,
But in vain; he is crushed by the felloe-rim;
The worm asks what can be overheard,

And wriggles deep from a scene so grim,
And guesses him safe; for he does not know
What a foul red flood will be soaking him!

Beaten about by the heel and toe
Are butterflies, sick of the day's long rheum
To die of a worse than the weather-foe.

Trodden and bruised to a miry tomb
Are ears that have greened but will never be gold,
And flowers in the bud that will never bloom.

So the season's intent, ere its fruit unfold,
Is frustrate, and mangled, and made succumb,
Like a youth of promise struck stark and cold! . . .

And what of these who to-night have come?
The young sleep sound; but the weather awakes
In the veterans, pains from the past that numb;

Old stabs of Ind, old Peninsular aches,
Old Friedland chills, haunt their moist mud bed,
Cramps from Austerlitz; till their slumber breaks.

And each soul shivers as sinks his head
On the loam he's to lease with the other dead
From tomorrow's mist-fall till Time be sped!

A Sheep Fair

The day arrives of the autumn fair,
     And torrents fall,
Though sheep in throngs are gathered there,
     Ten thousand all,
Sodden, with hurdles round them reared:
And, lot by lot, the pens are cleared,
And the auctioneer wrings out his beard,
And wipes his book, bedrenched and smeared,
And rakes the rain from his face with the edge of his hand,
     As torrents fall.

The wool of the ewes is like a sponge
     With the daylong rain:
Jammed tight, to turn, or lie, or lunge,
     They strive in vain.
Their horns are soft as finger-nails,
Their shepherds reek against the rails,
The tied dogs soak with tucked-in tails,
The buyers' hat-brims fill like pails,
Which spill small cascades when they shift their stand
     In the daylong rain.

A Note on Thomas Hardy

Thomas Hardy (1840–1928), English novelist and poet, born at Upper Bockhampton, near Dorchester, son of a master mason. He was educated at a private school near his home and from 1856 to 1861 was apprenticed to a church architect in Dorchester. In 1862 he went to London and worked under Sir Arthur Blomfield on church restoration (a subject which figures in several of his novels). At the same time he attended evening classes at King's College, studying Greek, Latin, theology, and astronomy as well as literature. In 1863 he was awarded prizes by the Royal Institute of British Architects. His earliest known piece of writing appeared in *Chambers' Journal*, 1865, under the title *How I Built Myself a House*. When in 1874 he married Emma Lavinia Gifford, their home at Max Gate near Dorchester was built to his own design.

During his time in London Hardy had written a number of poems but, finding no audience, he began to sketch fiction, an early composition being *The Poor Man and the Lady*, 1867. His first completed novel, *Desperate Remedies*, 1871, a murder story published at his own expense, contains elements of the astonishing and the incredible which in his later work took the form of a more sustained tension. The three novels that followed – *A Pair of Blue Eyes*, 1872–73, *Under the Greenwood Tree*, 1872, and *Far From the Madding Crowd*, 1874 – give vivid scenes of provincial life, especially the last where the shepherd Gabriel Oak is the first of a long line of characters who seem to 'grow out of' their rustic background. *The Hand of Ethelberta*, 1876, deals with high life in the city. *The Return of the Native*, published two years later, marks a major step forward in Hardy's development, being a highly charged novel in which the vast brooding expanse of Egdon Heath is said to be the real hero. *The Trumpet Major*, 1880, and *A Laodicean*, 1881, are unremarkable, but *The Mayor of Casterbridge*, 1886, is shaped round a penetrating study of the character of Michael Henchard. *The Woodlanders*, 1887, gives a sensitive picture of the rhythmic life of a tree-cutting, fence-making community and was followed by his most famous book, *Tess of the D'Urbervilles*, 1891. This challenged current ideas of respectability and aroused much hostile criticism, but the elemental qualities of Tess, as with many of Hardy's other heroines, give the book an energy that forces narrower moral considerations into a secondary place. *Jude the Obscure*, 1896, aroused even more widespread disgust and was labelled in some quarters 'Jude the Obscene'. It is a grim study of the downward path of an intelligent and sensitive young man, the bitter crushing of one aspiration after another, ending in a tragedy that spreads far beyond himself – a process that is presented as inevitable and beyond his control in the face of an enveloping and hostile fate. Its reception led Hardy to abandon novel-writing, though *The Well-Beloved*, a rather muddled fantasy, appeared in 1897. He also wrote four volumes of short stories; *Wessex Tales*, 1888; *A Group of Noble Dames*, 1891; *Life's Little Ironies*, 1894; and *A Changed Man*, 1913. Many of his short stories are masterly. From 1904 to 1908 he was engaged on *The Dynasts*, an epic drama in which war, national power, and political figures of Napoleonic times are represented as seen from above by supernatural spectators, or as Hardy called them 'certain impersonated abstractions and intelligences called spirits' who act as a commenting chorus. His only other dramatic piece is about the legend of Tristan and Isolde called *The Tragedy of the Queen of Cornwall*, 1923.

In his later years Hardy turned his literary energies to his first interest, poetry. Much early work is included in his first published volume, *Wessex Poems*, 1898. The rest of his poetry is contained in six volumes; *Poems of the Past and Present*, 1901; *Time's Laughing Stocks*, 1909; *Satires of Circumstance*, 1914; *Late Lyrics and Earlier*, 1922; *Human Shows*, 1925; and *Winter Words*, 1928. Altogether he wrote nearly 1000 poems, many of which are now rated more highly than even his best prose fiction. His first marriage was unhappy and those poems written about his wife after her death have an intensity and remorse that make them memorable, while many of his nature poems show the acute observation of the true countryman. There are interesting thematic links with the novels. In the latter he dramatises with uncompromising directness a belief in the futility of fighting against the cruelties of circumstance, the inevitability of each man's destiny, and the passing of all beauty. 'I should like flowers very much if I didn't keep on thinking they would all be withered in a few days' says Little Father Time in *Jude the Obscure*. The poems often contain a compressed version of the same theme, either by seeing ahead from a happy present to a grim future or else looking back from the bitterness of the present to a past that was full of promise.